I0421103

TABLE OF CONTENTS

THE CONSTITUTION OF INDIA   2

THE CONSTITUTION OF INDIA IS A "HOLY COW"   2
THE PRINCIPAL-AGENT PROBLEM IN GOVERNANCE   7
"RULE OF LAW"... FOR INDIA   14

CRIMINAL JUSTICE SYSTEM   22

AN INDIAN'S DAILY EXPERIENCE OF THE LAW   22
POLICE REFORMS: OUTRUNNING THE PAST   29
ACCESS TO THE CRIMINAL JUSTICE SYSTEM IN INDIA   41

POLICE REFORMS   55

POLICING WITHOUT USING FORCE: "JALPAIGURI EXPERIMENT"   55
THE POLICE STATION AT THE VANGUARD: TRAINING OF
OFFICERS-IN-CHARGE AND ADDITIONAL OFFICERS-IN-CHARGE OF
POLICE STATIONS IN KOLKATA BY IIM ALUMNI   94
CENTRALIZING THE INVESTIGATION FUNCTION   147

OTHER ESSAYS   151

OPPORTUNITY FOR BIHAR   151
A KEMALIST VISION FOR PAKISTAN   156
USD DOWNGRADE - OPPORTUNITY INR   162

The Constitution of India is a "holy cow"

"I am increasingly persuaded that the earth belongs exclusively to the living and that one generation has no more right to bind another to its laws and judgments than one independent nation has the right to command another." – Thomas Jefferson

The Constitution of India is the longest written constitution of any sovereign state in the world. In spite of the verbosity of its constitution, India is home to the world's largest number of illiterate persons (United Nations Development Programme (UNDP) Report 2011). Despite some recent economic advances, this state presents a Greek tragedy of stone-hearted indifference to arguably the largest number of disadvantaged people in a country.

The author asserts with confidence that there no one in the world who has read the entire Constitution of India with all its 448 articles in 24 parts, 12 schedules and 97 amendments from cover to cover.

The reason is simple. It is not such a readable document.

Some assertive ones will contest the above claim and seek to browbeat the author with their intellectual prowess. They will claim that they have completely and continuously read the Constitution of India... these are bureaucrats, judges, members of the Parliament of India...who are paid public money to make a career out of reading, interpreting and occasionally changing the constitution.

The Constitution of India remains like the proverbial elephant being touched in different parts by many blind men, coming up with their own interpretation of the nature of the creature. There has been a running debate on the "basic structure" of this document for pretty much since its inception, including a landmark Supreme Court judgement in 1973.

This is the unwieldy and incomprehensible Rule Book that is supposed to guide the daily lives of the people of India and their municipalities, state and federal governments and the relations between them. No wonder no one really knows what is going on in India, except those who claim special knowledge or forbearance, of which unfortunately there is quite a few. And no wonder the country's progress is being held back because there is no unanimity of understanding on the set of rules.

Obfuscation of the rules, deliberate or accidental, plays into the hands of a government and bureaucracy keen to exercise and perpetuate its rule over the people. Successive amendments have progressively diluted, restricted and sometimes abrogated, the original "Fundamental Rights" of the citizen enshrined in the constitution in 1949. Of course it is all done in the name of the betterment of the people who are thus shackled.

Contrast the ninety seven times amended Constitution of India with the constitution of the United States. The American has been amended a total of twenty seven times in its history. Successive amendments have upheld the inviolate nature of the freedom of the citizen. As a matter of fact the first ten amendments to the American Constitution are called the "Bill of Rights" which strengthen individual rights vis a vis the government and law makers.

Is it at all possible that Indians deserve to give themselves a Constitution, the Rule Book to run their lives, which can be bedtime reading at most? A document which can be explained succinctly and simply by those who have read it, to those who do not know how to read?

The above rhetorical questions, the author believes, need to be answered quickly in the affirmative, not only for the world's largest democracy to amble along at a faster clip, but also to effectively reverse the centuries old degradation of the average disadvantaged Indian.

The Principal-Agent problem in governance

It is time that Indians wake up to the fact that they are quite far from enjoying real personal, economic and political freedom. Realization is the first step to rectification.

Typically a lot of care is taken in appointing and supervising our agents or vendors in different facets of our life. Imagine the kind of effort we take when recruiting, appraising and promoting or dismissing at our workplaces and maybe more so at home. But, paradoxically, in appointing the people who run our governments, and even less so in monitoring them, we have little teeth. Principles of people management, so pervasive in all other aspects, go out of the window when it comes to appointing and running our governments.

The nomenclature "Representation of the People Act" is puzzling. It appears that the people being one of the major stake-holders; are being represented in the process of appointment of governments. It reads as if, and probably is, that the powers that be have benevolently given representation to the people also among other stakeholders.

A casual Google search throws light on this matter. "The Representation of the People Act" was given the royal accent of His Majesty George V, King of the United Kingdom, in 1918 to enfranchise a greater number of his adult subjects as part of the fourth phase of electoral reforms. This was a grateful monarch's largesse to his subjects for loyally defending his crown and realm from the Huns.

This action seems to have been copied by the new rulers of India when the President signed into law "The Representation of People Act" of 1951. Universal suffrage was granted to the entire adult population, which allowed them to vote in elections periodically on the principles of "one man one vote" and "first past the post". We find that a number of people, particularly in urban areas, did not vote, treating election dates as forced holidays. Such people intuitively may have realized that the voting process is more an exercise of legitimizing the regime's authority. It is far from being a clear and robust process of appointment of agents by the people, who are the principals.

One would much rather propose that we give ourselves an "Appointment of the Government Act". This change in terminology would put the principal-agent relationship in the right perspective. The paramount authority of the people over the government may thus be made clear.

It is the thesis of this article that currently the people are ruled by the government, which legitimizes its position periodically through a balloting process. Elections have been used in every time and country to legitimize authority. Hitler was the elected leader of Germany, as also were several other heads of government of dubious distinction. Democracy clearly is essential, but not enough.

There is an entity called the government of India, with vast land holdings, majority shareholding in massive corporations, owning almost all infrastructural assets, conducting foreign relations and engaging in deficit financing by printing money. In effect, ruling India. Besides the politicians, the civil services - modelled on that of the imperial Chinese bureaucracy, crony capitalists, family members and friends are beneficiaries and stakeholders of this setup. The system of extraction of resources from this country has been fine tuned over two centuries of British rule and was pretty much taken over lock stock and barrel when they left. In terms of cash flows, while earlier the bounty from the colonies used to flow to the metropole, nowadays the same is placed under custody of crony capitalists or moves into the international private banking system. Such an arrangement is detrimental to the national interest.

Coming to the accountability and expectations from our agents, the principals, that is, Indians, do not have oversight over the conduct of their agents, once the election process is over.

We do not have a "Monitoring the Government Act" or a "Appraisal and Dismissal of the Government Act" to do exactly what the wording suggests, that is, watch over and guide the working of the agents, at every step, and possibly asking them to step aside if they do not make the mark. It is unthinkable for Indians, used to millennia of servitude, to even imagine that they have a right of oversight over those who rule them. So far, post elections, it is pretty much a free run for law makers and that small group who comprise the executive. The work and workings of government is opaque to the ordinary citizen.

There is little effective supervision of the actions and motivations of the executive by institutional watchdogs, other than an occasional CAG report or a CBI enquiry, or judicial activism. All these actions, if they happen in some cases, are post-facto, after the damage to the national interest has already been done. Criminal proceedings against the guilty, does not even begin to recover the socio-economic cost of their actions.

It is a cosy situation for the bureaucracy, colloquially referred to as Indian Automatic Service. They enjoy job security time bound promotion and enjoyment of resources far in excess of their contribution, irrespective of the outcome of elections or the state of affairs in the country.

Large numbers of educated and skilled Indians, who have chosen, or could not become part of the establishment, have immigrated to other countries, apparently in search of a better quality of life. In their home country they may have found the lack of freedom stifling.

This is a diagnostic, no solutions are proposed.

To hark back to Abraham Lincoln's Gettysburg address, "government of the people, by the people, for the people, shall not perish from the earth." Indians have a long road to travel, difficult choices to make and radically change long-held attitudes and assumptions. Until and unless the people proactively appoint, guide, monitor and dismiss governments, those in power will continue to extract and exploit. It is right and essential to upgrade and professionalize governance, so that the people of India finally become free.

"Rule of Law"… for India

The Universal Declaration of Human Rights states: "…so that people are not compelled to rebellion against tyranny, human rights should be protected by rule of law…"

The ancient concept of "rule of law" is separate from rule *by* law. Under the "rule of law" the law is preeminent and serves as a check against the abuse of power by the executive. Under "rule by law", the law can serve as a mere tool for a government that suppresses in a legalistic fashion. For example Nazi Germany acted as per laws enacted by the German Reichstag in conducting the holocaust of Jews and South Africa's apartheid laws were also promulgated by its legislature. Just and good laws are therefore a prerequisite for "rule of law".

Plato wrote: "Where the law is subject to some other authority and has none of its own, the collapse of the state, in my view, is not far off; but if law is the master of the government and the government is its slave, then the situation is full of promise and men enjoy all the blessings that the gods shower on a state." Indeed "rule of law" and per capita income has a direct and strong correlation.

The World Justice Project (WJP), a Washington based think tank, has recently published its third "Rule of Law Index". Thirty five countries are benchmarked with regard to nine factors illustrating "rule of law" in their respective jurisdictions. The WJP's index is the only such instrument addressing this subject.

The WJP index for India gives the opportunity to interested persons to use it as a diagnostic tool.

In terms of regional ranking in South Asia, India's western neighbour is the only other respondent. Predictably so, India outranks this neighbour on every factor. This is hardly a matter for self-congratulation though for the world's largest functioning democracy, given that the western neighbour is a basket case as a nation state.

On a cursory study of the "Global Ranking" and Income Group Ranking" of the index certain conclusions emerge.

Firstly, India scores high on "Limited Government Powers", "Clear, Publicized and Stable Laws" and "Open Government", being ranked number one on these factors in its "Income Group" ranking. This is more a tribute to the founding fathers of the Indian Republic who framed the Constitution, than to their successors. Of course, on these factors, India just about makes the top ten globally, which points to scope for improvement, for India to create a community of real equity and opportunity for its citizens.

Secondly, India's poor showing in "Absence of Corruption" is insightful into why a country with such an enlightened and sophisticated system of governance has performed indifferently in delivering to its citizens. Indeed the great strain, under which Indian society labours, can be linked not to the lack of democratic institutions, but to their abuse by the persons who are their stewards.

More troubling are the rest of the factors, which deal with the Indian citizen's daily experience of "rule of law".

Poor show on "Order and Security" and "Regulatory Enforcement" point to serious malaise in governance and threat to internal security. Coupled with the subversion by rent-seeking of India's democratic institutions, one feels that, in the absence of upright and clear leadership the enforcers of "rule of law" are handicapped in their functioning. Also it possibly is that interested parties have conspired to keep the enforcers of the law moribund and enfeebled.

No doubt the indifferent score on "Fundamental Rights" is an outcome of the above situation.

Low scoring on "Access to Civil Justice" and "Effective Criminal Justice" are matters of grave concern. The first purpose of the state is to deliver justice. India is faltering in that aspect.

Current laws and regulations themselves give rise to doubt regarding their justness and relevance, given that the main bodies of legislation and procedures governing civil and criminal justice systems are hand-me-downs from the mid-nineteenth century British colonial era! Since independence, law-makers seemed to have had little time to craft just and good laws relevant to the requirements of a free people. This indeed makes the Constitution of 1950 the exotic topping of a cake whose crust comprise of the musty Indian Penal Code of 1860; The Indian Police Act of 1861, The Criminal Procedure Code of 1898 (amended piecemeal since then); The Indian Evidence Act of 1872 and the Civil Procedure Code circa 1908. These pieces of legislation surely were good laws in their times for colonial rulers and local elites, but may just have outlived their relevance and scope in changed times and circumstances.

For example, sentences for crimes are relatively severe. The accused therefore naturally fights tooth and nail to avoid indictment, and the weakest sections of society have a greater chance of being convicted and going to jail. Sentencing needs to become light and fast, with the intention of correction and not retribution.

The police infrastructure of India remains as it was designed by colonial rulers in the nineteenth century to control large native populations. By accident or design this infrastructure's capabilities have not been substantially augmented.

Such are some conclusions that can be readily drawn from the WJP's "Rule of Law" index for India. Much of this was known, but now there is a quantitative tool available to validate intuitive hypotheses. The need for reforms is urgent and the

agenda is large, but needs to be undertaken nonetheless in the

national interest.

The World Justice Project's "Rule of Law" Index for India

Score	Global Ranking	Regional Ranking	Income Group Ranking
Factor 1: Limited Government Powers	14/ 35	1/ 2	1/ 12
Factor 2: Absence of Corruption	25/ 35	1/ 2	7/ 12
Factor 3: Clear, Publicized, and Stable Laws	13/ 35	1/ 2	1/ 12
Factor 4: Order and Security	23/ 35	1/ 2	8/ 12
Factor 5: Fundamental Rights	20/ 35	1/ 2	4/ 12
Factor 6: Open Government	9/ 35	1/ 2	1/ 12
Factor 7: Regulatory Enforcement	24/ 35	1/ 2	9/ 12
Factor 8: Access to Civil Justice	27/ 35	1/ 2	8/ 12
Factor 9: Effective Criminal Justice	23/ 35	1/ 2	7/ 12

An Indian's daily experience of the Law

India is the largest and probably the greatest functioning democracy in the world today and every Indian should derive legitimate pride and satisfaction from such a situation.

The Indian citizen votes typically every five years. Candidates are elected as lawmakers, and lawmakers from the political party getting higher votes occupy the executive positions. The judiciary is independent from the executive and legislature and the Supreme Court does a neat job of upholding Fundamental Rights guaranteed by the Constitution.

Despite the structural sophistication and robustness of the Indian state, the citizen's daily experience of the Law is not so happy.

The principal code of criminal legislation in India is the Indian Penal Code of 1860. This code listed all possible criminal offences which could be committed in British India, in the years following the abortive First War of Independence. The punishment for petty theft is imprisonment for three years. This was probably an improvement over whipping, which was common at that time, but definitely too strict in these times. Laws that seek retribution rather than correction, and impose harsh punishment, force the accused to fight tooth and nail for acquittal. The jails today, which incidentally have been renamed Correction Centres in different Indian states, are full of under-trials and a few unfortunate members of the weaker sections, who did not possess the knowledge or funds to escape conviction.

The legislation which provides the police forces its power and organization is the Indian Police Act of 1861. The aim of this act was to empower a limited constabulary to control a large and potentially restive native population. The colonial police had carried out some of the harshest attacks on civil liberties at that time. Independent India has retained this piece of legislation, which defines policing today. The police infrastructure envisaged under this act has absolutely failed to keep up with growing population and changing crime brought about by economic growth, technological change, urbanization and internal migration. Both individual police officers and other stakeholders are unable to bridge the gaps in internal security and law and order which results from such strain. Growing insurgency in different parts of India forces the central government to provide paramilitary support to the state police. It is probably an easier solution to empower and strengthen the police to an extent that they can effectively ensure the citizen's access to criminal justice and also effectively ensure internal security.

The criminal justice system of the country is dependent on the Criminal Procedure Code of 1898 for the administration of criminal justice. This nineteenth century dinosaur was supposedly substantially revised in 1973, but the author doubts if it has fully metamorphosed into a creature of the twenty first century. The CrPC 1973 empowers the Station House Officer (SHO) of each Police Station with draconian powers of search and arrest and expects the SHO to be an avatar of Solomon in terms of his discretion in ensuring justice and fair play. Prior to independence, per chance if the SHO fell short of such expectation, surely the colonial rulers were not too perturbed with resultant human rights violations and injustice meted out to the colonized. In independent India, the public continues to fear and misunderstand the SHO, while the SHO, in spite of best efforts, often falls short of expectations owing to constraint of resources and the bindings of archaic procedures. The author feels that free citizens of India do not require such a situation to continue.

The Indian Evidence Act of 1872 provides the legal background for acceptance of evidence. Since there was no e-mail, facsimile, world wide web, X-rays, scanners or cameras...

still and video, in 1878, this act is technologically obsolete. This obsolescence has led to the Indian law courts being the most congested in the world. Justice delayed is justice denied... that's the reality of the justice system of India today.

The civil courts depend on the Civil Procedure Code of 1908 to administer civil justice. The Constitution of India enjoins the courts and law enforcement officers to follow the "procedure as laid down by law" and not "due process of the law" as is the case in the United States. The complicated procedures make Indian civil justice one of the weakest in the world. The judge may also intuitively know that the accused is innocent, but has to pass a sentence of conviction, because as per the procedure laid down by the law the accused is guilty.

The above are the five pillars of the civil and criminal justice system of India, as well as the basis for the enforcement of law and maintenance of internal security. Combined with such systemic weakness, is the lack of effort in educating the citizen about the law. An Indian school child's education starts and stops with a study of the hallowed tenets of the Constitution. However the citizen is impacted by the important pieces of legislation in daily life, which is not part of the educational curriculum of the ordinary citizen. Highly educated people in India are completely ignorant and confused about how the law works for or against them in daily life.

Unless the pivotal pieces of legislation are reframed and reshaped in keeping with the requirements of a free people of the twenty first century, "rule of law" will continue to be compromised in India. The Constitution of India will remain the palatable icing on a cake whose crust comprising of five principal pieces of legislation has gone bad a long time back. Important twentieth century developments such as the "Universal Declaration of Human Rights" of 1948 have bypassed India, since the most important pieces of legislation were drafted before the enlightened proclamations of the last century.

It is time that just, good, clear and well publicized laws are crafted through the democratic process. Only then will Indians truly enjoy the Indian state's contract with its people as promised and envisioned by the founding fathers of the Constituent Assembly of 1949.

Police Reforms: Outrunning the past

Organized policing in India started with Charles Napier, who, in 1842, at the age of 60, was appointed to command the British Indian army of Bombay Presidency.

An army man, Napier had spent many years in the beginning of his career fighting Napoleon's legions on the Iberian Peninsula. In 1843, Napier marched to Sindh at the head of his army, to put down rebellions by the local chieftains. He did so, and then went further.

Blatantly disregarding treaty obligations with the independent Sindhi chieftains and technically being insubordinate to his bosses, he ended up conquering and annexing the entire province to British India. After the job, he dispatched to his superiors the short message, "Peccavi", Latin for "I have sinned" (a pun on I have Sindh).

Proponents of British rule over India justified the conquest thus: "If this was a piece of rascality, it was a noble piece of rascality!"

An army officer towards the end of his career, Napier was then burdened with the job of administering an ill-gotten possession. Concerned with subduing rebellious chieftains and keeping the disgruntled native population in check, he got together disbanded and retired army officers to form a provincial constabulary.

He improvised on his job, with an ad hoc approach.

A story for which he is noted deals with Hindus complaining about prohibition of Sati: "You say that it is your custom to burn widows. Very well. We also have a custom: when men burn a woman alive, we tie a rope around their necks and we hang them. Build your funeral pyre; [then] beside it, my carpenters will build a gallows. You may follow your custom. And then we will follow ours."

Napier's perspectives on policing are shown through the following comments: "The best way to quiet a country is a good thrashing, followed by great kindness afterwards. Even the wildest chaps are thus tamed" and "the human mind is never better disposed to gratitude and attachment than when softened by fear." His model was successful since "fear" and loathing are the key emotions that Indians felt regarding the police.

The policing system in the provinces of British India, instituted then, and which unfortunately has continued till date, was marked by the imperialist prerogative of maintaining control by a relatively small constabulary over large native populations. The police became the important tool of the state for keeping an oppressed native population in submission. It was not the priority of colonial rulers to administer the Criminal

Justice System for the common man, let alone bother much about the niceties of protection of human rights of their native subjects.

The beginning made by Napier in Sindh was later codified into the Police Act of 1861 and the Indian Penal Code of 1860.

Maja Daruwala and others of the Commonwealth Human Rights Initiative wrote: "The Police Act, 1861 was legislated by the British in the aftermath of the Mutiny of 1857 or the First War of Independence. The British, naturally at that time wanted to establish a police force that would suit the purpose of crushing dissent and any movement for self government."

Intelligence gathering to forestall moves towards independence was an important job of the police.

Sir John Hunt, leader of the successful 1953 British Expedition to Mount Everest, was a Military Intelligence officer in the Indian Army, and was seconded to the Indian police. Hunt worked undercover, gathering intelligence in Chittagong whilst dressed in Indian clothing. This was just after the Chittagong armory raid, an attempt in 1930 to raid the armory of police and auxiliary forces, by revolutionary freedom fighters led by Surya Sen. "Hunter sahib" contributed to the arrest of many revolutionaries for which he was awarded the Indian police medal.

The emergence of India as an independent nation state was long and rough with the price being paid in blood. Predictably the Imperial Police played a noteworthy role in trying to stymie the legitimate struggle of the Indian people.

The Dandi March and the ensuing Dharasana Satyagraha drew worldwide attention to the Indian independence movement through extensive newspaper and newsreel coverage.

In 1930 the Indian National Congress chose satyagraha as their main tactic for winning independence from British rule and appointed Gandhi to organize the campaign. Gandhi chose the 1882 British Salt Act as the first target of satyagraha. The Salt March to Dandi, and the beating by police of hundreds of nonviolent protesters received worldwide news coverage. United Press correspondent Webb Miller reported that:

"Not one of the marchers even raised an arm to fend off the blows. They went down like ten-pins. From where I stood I heard the sickening whacks of the clubs on unprotected skulls. The waiting crowd of watchers groaned and sucked in their breaths in sympathetic pain at every blow. Those struck down fell sprawling, unconscious or writhing in pain with fractured skulls or broken shoulders. In two or three minutes the ground was quilted with bodies. Great patches of blood widened on their white clothes. The survivors without breaking ranks silently and doggedly marched on until struck down."

Vithalbhai Patel, former Speaker of the Assembly, watched the beatings and remarked, "All hope of reconciling India with the British Empire is lost forever."

Following attempts by the British to censor Miller's story, it eventually appeared in 1,350 newspapers throughout the world, and was read into the official record of the United States Senate. Time magazine declared Gandhi its 1930 Man of the Year, comparing Gandhi's march to the sea "to defy Britain's salt tax as some New Englanders once defied a British tea tax."

It is strange that those at the receiving end of the lathis and bullets of the Imperial Police did nothing to change the repressive nature of policing after India became free.

The Midnapore region of West Bengal, of Lalgarh and Nandigram fame, does have a history of parallel governments.

Such a parallel government, from Tamluk town in Midnapore, functioned from 1942 to 1944 as part of the Quit India Movement.

To set up such a government, members of the Indian National Congress planned to take over the various police stations and other government offices as a step to overthrowing the British. Matangini Hazra, who was 73 years at the time, led a procession of six thousand, mostly unarmed women volunteers, towards the police station in Tamluk.

The marchers were ordered to disband and then fired upon. As she stepped forward, Matangini Hazra was shot once. She continued to advance with the tri-color, leaving other volunteers behind. The police shot her three times. As she was repeatedly shot, she kept chanting Vande Mataram and died with the flag held high and still flying.

The country was independent and Matangini Hazra was honored by a spate of road-naming and unveiling of statues. However, nothing was done to align the police forces, the hated instrument of oppression of the British Raj, with the needs of a self-governing people.

The country had to wait till 1977 for the first step towards police reforms until the first Janata Dal government was formed.

In the years of Emergency, the political opposition was subjected to unprecedented police brutality. Serving and retired officers of the Indian Police Service were appalled at the misuse of the police forces by the vested political interests. Their clamor for police reforms was given a sympathetic ear by Chaudhary Charan Singh, the Home Minister. He instituted the first commission for Police Reforms.

The first Janata Dal government did not last long enough to implement the commission's recommendations. Subsequently several other commissions submitted their reports on the same subject, which gathered dust. It seemed that the police forces were the instrument of oppression by the ruling class over the common citizen of India.

Panning to the first decade of twenty first century India, we find that a gentleman named Prakash Singh took up the cudgels for police reforms. Having been Director General of Police of Uttar Pradesh and thereafter having headed the police of ULFA-affected Assam, he had all the right credentials as a policeman.

He filed a PIL in the Supreme Court praying for implementation of police reforms. The Supreme Court ruled in his favor, asking the states to legislate new police acts. Horror of horrors, some states passed acts which are even more retrograde than the earlier Police Act of 1861.

This leaves us today with a over-stretched police force with archaic infrastructure, training, manpower, equipment and mindset... ill-equipped to meet the needs of the civil society of the world's largest democracy.

While a significant percentage of the country's resources, and very rightly so, is devoted to the armed forces, one tends to forget that today wars are fought more often than not within the nation's borders. It is the police which are charged with internal security.

Occasionally an Ajmal Kasab forces kneejerk reactions. But is it that we should depend solely on people of his ilk to reactively force us into modernizing our police forces? Can we, as a people, not muster the genius to devise the policing that we need and deserve?

These are questions we need to answer fast to decisively move into the era of Pax Indica that beckons us in the years to come.

Access to the Criminal Justice System in India

Background

The reality of non-registration of FIRs (burking) has plagued Indian society since 1861 when organized policing was instituted by the British. From a preliminary understanding it appears that the policing system as instituted then, and which unfortunately has continued till date, by General Sir Charles Napier, the conqueror and administrator of Sindh, was marked by the imperialist prerogative of maintaining control by a relatively small constabulary over large native populations. Some telling comments on his perspective of policing, by Mr. Napier, are as follows: "The best way to quiet a country is a good thrashing, followed by great kindness afterwards. Even the wildest chaps are thus tamed" and "the human mind is never better disposed to gratitude and attachment than when softened by fear." Obviously such statements made by the founder of policing in modern India, does little to inspire confidence in the infrastructure established by him. We reasonably suspect that it was not the priority of erstwhile colonial rulers to administer the Criminal Justice System for the common man in British India, let alone bother much about the niceties of protection of human rights of their then colonial subjects.

Post independence, India, while grappling with developmental and external security issues, has not done much to set things right on the policing front.

The Police is the first bulwark of the Criminal Justice System. Every citizen has the constitutional right to record a complaint of cognizable offence with the police. Unfortunately, as a ballpark, it is estimated that on an average only 2 out of a possible 100 complaints are registered by the police in India.

Constitutional Position

U/s 154 Cr.P.C. states: "Every information relating to the commission of a cognizable offence, if given orally to an Officer-in-charge of a Police Station, shall be reduced to writing by him or under his direction, and be read over to the informant; and every such information, whether given in writing or reduced to writing as aforesaid, shall be signed by the person giving it, and the substance thereof shall be entered in a book to be kept by such officer in such form as the State Government may prescribe in this behalf."

The police forces are been mandated to implement the law by following its procedure. Every law has its own course/procedure. The legislature, at the Centre and the States, make the laws. The police are not competent to change the processes of law, neither are they supposed to stop or alter them. However, when it comes to freely registering FIRs, many honest and upright police officers find entirely honorable excuses to not register them.

The Hon'ble Supreme Court pronouncements: (Kuldip Singh –vs- State 1994 Cr.L.J. 1502, Rashtriya Mukthi Morcha –vs- Suraj Mandal 1996(38) D.R.J 250 (DB).and many others....) "The Police is bound to register the information received of commission of cognizable offence unless the information is vague, incomplete or does not disclose cognizable offence". The police officer may be sent to jail in case of refusal of FIR - SC WRIT PETITION CRL. NO.68 OF 2008 dt 14/07/2008.

"In case F.I.R.s are not registered within the aforementioned time, and/or aforementioned steps are not taken by the police, the concerned Magistrate would be justified in initiating contempt proceeding against such delinquent officers and punish them for violation of its orders if no sufficient cause is shown and awarding stringent punishment like sentence of imprisonment against them inasmuch as the Disciplinary Authority would be quite justified in initiating departmental proceeding and suspending them in contemplation of the same."

Ideal vs Reality

Superiors would tend to judge their junior officers on the number of cases outstanding, which incentivizes the SHO and Duty Officer from not recording or understating the commission of cognizable offences. India today has 166 cases registered in a year on average per 100,000 people as opposed to upwards of 7,500 cases in any developed country.

This has helped the offenders or criminals only; alienated the public from the police and given scope to outsiders to interfere. Respect and fear of law has gone away, the Criminal Justice System is being seen as a farce and lawlessness has become the hallmark of our society.

As knee-jerk reactions Commission after other has been constituted to fight for the rights of perceived weaker sections of our polity. They have passed their own set of laws, which are again dependent on enforcement by the same police forces, whose capabilities have not been bolstered with regard to changing times and the needs and expectations of a democratic society.

The obstruction to the citizens' access to the Criminal Justice System over generations has many proliferated many ills, including the penetration of Maoists in the so-called Red Corridor.

We feel that free access of ordinary citizens to the Criminal Justice System through the route of free recording of FIRs at Police Stations, will effectively battle many malignancies in our polity and firmly establish and uphold the rule of law required by a democratic and modern civil society.

Police Reforms?

Police reforms were sought to be undertaken in India from 1977 onwards, when the then Home Minister, Ch Charan Singh constituted the first of 13 such Commissions for this purpose. We had to wait till 2006 for some states to legislate new police acts, which, horror of horrors, are sometimes more retrograde than the earlier act, going against the spirit of the Soli Sorabjee Committee, which recommended such new legislation.

New Challenges

In the meantime, the security challenge has now shifted from the country's borders in the form of terrorism sponsored by hostile countries, in-house divisive forces, extreme left-wing insurgency, irresponsible political activism and caste and religion based politics. This combines with corruption and white-collar crime to create a vitriolic challenge for policing today.

For reasons which require deeper exploration, the Police infrastructure has not received the incremental resource allocation, technology up-gradation and training that it desperately needs to meet contemporary challenges. For example the DRDO (the research wing of the Ministry of Defense) has an annual budget in excess of INR 100 Cr, while the BPRD (Bureau of Police Research and Development) has around INR 5 Cr at its disposal annually.

Police continues to be on the State list. This has literally meant that the Home Ministry of GOI has no direct control over the police forces. However, there are six paramilitary forces reporting to this ministry, which are regularly engaged in backing up the police in areas where critical challenges are being faced.

Maybe it would make greater sense for our polity to enhance the capabilities of the police forces, so that they have enough resources to meet internal security challenges effectively.

Initiatives towards 100% registration of FIRs

Over the years, several idealistic police officers have been seeking to implement 100% registration of FIRs in their respective jurisdictions, with varying levels of success. We have observed that the experiment in Jalpaiguri, West Bengal, in 2007-08, by the then SP, Tripurari Sharma IPS, has been the strongest and most credible effort so far. He has since then sought to replicate the success in Kolkata Police as DC Eastern Suburban Division and now as DC Central Division.

Some other such initiatives have been by Sh Nilabh Kishore IPS, in Fatehgarh Sahib, Punjab in 2007-08, Sh N.K. Shinghal (Retd.) IPS in Delhi. It is important that such individual initiatives now take on an institutionalized character across the more than 600 districts of India.

Obstacles

Some obvious problem areas for implementation are shortage of investigative personnel and pileup of cases in the judiciary. The 100% registration of FIRs will necessarily set in motion the process of reasonable allocation of resources to the police forces and other reforms based on the actual crime situation in the country. The upshot is we will emerge as a modern society with modern policing in place.

Benefits observed in Jalpaiguri District

With the free registration of cases, there is no discrimination between rich and poor. It has induced a change in the behavioral pattern of the police officers as they are not indulging in atrocities, misbehavior, intimidation, etc. Police is using FIR as a potent weapon to wrestle with crime and to maintain peace and tranquility.

Police has become the protector of human rights. The mental trauma of police officers, due to suppression/minimization of cases, has gone away. The impact on law and order of the district is positive because of the effective implementation of the law.

Some Persons interviewed

- Sh Asok Mohan Chakraborty, (Retd.) IAS, Former Home Secretary, GoWB

- Sh A.B. Vohra, (Retd.) IPS, Former DGP, West Bengal

- Sh Arun Prosad Mukherjee, (Retd.) IPS, Former DGP, West Bengal and ex-Governor of Meghalaya

- Sh Bhupinder Singh, IPS, DGP, West Bengal

- Sh Arvind Verma (Retd.) IPS

- Dr. Ashok Dhamija (Retd.) IPS

- Sh N. Narasimhan, (Retd.) IPS

- Sh N.K. Shinghal, (Retd.) IPS

- Sh Amitabh Thakur, IPS, UP

- Sh Kamal Kumar (Retd.) IPS

- Sh Ramakrishnan, (Retd.) IPS

- Sh Ashish Gupta, IPS, UP

- Sh RJS Nalwa, IPS, West Bengal

- Sh Adhir Sharma, IPS, West Bengal

- Sh Zulfiquar Hasan, IPS, West Bengal

- Sh Thayagaraju, IPS, West Bengal

- Sh Ranvir Kumar, IPS, West Bengal

- Sh Goutam Mohan Chakraborty, IPS, Commissioner of Police, Kolkata

- Sh Nandkumar Saravade, (Retd.) IPS

- Sh Nilabh Kishore, IPS, Punjab

- Sh Tripurari, IPS, DC Central Division, Kolkata Police

- Sh Anand Kumar, IPS, SP Jalpaiguri, West Bengal

- Sh Kalyan Bandopadhyay, IPS, SP Cooch Behar, West Bengal

- Sh Hari Kusumakar, IPS, SP Howrah, West Bengal

- Sh Manoj Kumar Verma, IPS, SP Medinipur West, West Bengal

- Sh R. Ranjit, IAS, West Bengal

- Smt Vandana Yadav, IAS, DM Jalpaiguri, West Bengal

- Sh Narayan Swarup Nigam IAS, DM West Midnapore, West Bengal

- Sh Saumitra Mohan IAS, DM Birbhum, West Bengal

- Sh Manohar Tirkey, MP, RSP, West Bengal

- Sh Debaprasad Ray, MLA, Jalpaiguri, West Bengal

- Sh Santosh Sarkar, Member, CPI(M) District Committee, Jalpaiguri, West Bengal

- Sh Tapan Bhattacharjee, Secretary, Bar Association, Jalpaiguri, West Bengal

- Sh P.K. Bhattacharjee, Secretary, Indian Tea Association, Dooars Branch

- Members of Judiciary who have chosen to remain anonymous

- Many SHOs and police personnel across several districts.

Policing without using force: "Jalpaiguri Experiment"

Advocacy Paper by Jhelum Chowdhury

The author has been working pro bono on Police Reforms since 2009.

From 2009-10, he led a team of IIM alumni in field study and extensive documentation of the "Jalpaiguri Experiment" conducted by Sh Tripurari, IPS, when he was SP of Jalpaiguri District, West Bengal, in 2007.

In short, the so-called "Jalpaiguri Experiment" focussed on complete enforcement of Sec 154 of the CrPC through 100% registration of all complaints received at Police Stations. It was the finding of the study that the law and order situation generally improved in Jalpaiguri district during and after that period, which could be directly correlated with the "Jalpaiguri Experiment"

The author is associated with the Takshashila Institution, a networked "Indian national interest" think tank and the World Justice Project, a Washington DC based NGO engaged in strengthening "rule of law".

He is an expert contributor to the World Justice Project's "Rule of Law Index".

Introduction

It is to the credit of the British that they introduced the concept of "rule of law" in India by setting up institutions such as the High Courts, the police forces, prison system and by enacting necessary legislation.

Independent India inherited British era laws in the form of the Indian Police Act of 1861, the Indian Penal Code of 1862, as well as the Criminal Procedure Code of 1898 (the CrPC) which provide the bulwark of "rule of law" in India.

Sadly the application of the"rule of law" was always and has still remained selective in nature. This selective application of the"rule of law" is seen by this report as the root cause of absence of social justice in India.

As India attained Independence, laws such as the Indian Police Act, the Indian Penal Code and the Criminal Procedure Code should have been replaced with something that reflected the desires of an independent nation. But successive governments in the last 63 years have chosen not to undertake reforms in the area of delivering criminal justice to the common citizen.

The First Information Report (FIR) is always the first step in launching a criminal investigation. In the police's refusal to register an FIR, the victim is denied the right to justice. Very few individuals in this country know that they can get an FIR registered through court and even if they do know about it, they usually have very little money to begin with, leave alone spend it on legal fees to get an FIR registered.

The refusal on the part of the police to register a cognizable offence is known in police parlance as "burking".

As defined in the CrPC, "A cognizable offence is one in which the police is empowered to register a FIR, investigate and arrest an accused involved in cognizable crime without a court warrant. A non-cognizable offence is one in which police can neither register a First Information Report (FIR) nor can investigate or effect arrest without the express permission or directions from the court."

Any meaningful police reform has to tackle "burking" effectively and give the victims of crime the ability to register an FIR without delay.

"Jalpaiguri Experiment"

In a noble initiative to tackle this problem, Mr. Tripurari IPS, conducted the "Jalpaiguri Experiment" (also referred to as Policing without using Force) while he was posted as the Superintendent of Police, Jalpaiguri, West Bengal in 2007-08. In his report on the experiment, Mr Tripurari stated that "the first and probably the most important stage where the"rule of law" stands negated is the time when the cognizable complaint is not registered at the police station, thereby endangering and compromising the right to life, liberty and honour of almost every individual."

Mr Tripurari ordered all the Station House Officers (the SHOs) in the police stations that came under his jurisdiction to register FIRs in all complaints of cognizable offences without going into the merits of the complaint at the time of recording of the FIR. This overturned the usual practice in India wherein merits of the complaint have to be established before an FIR is registered.

According to him, the experiment produced remarkable results and was "successful in curbing the menace of burking of crimes at the police stations and reduced to a great extent the misuse of power of arrest by the police." In an environment where police officers are punished for having too many pending cases, during the Jalpaiguri Experiment this concern was put aside by assuring the investigating officers that they still had to dispose of the same number of cases as they were disposing off prior to the start of the experiment.

Results of the experiment

As the experiment unfolded there was a uniform rise the registration of crime in all the seventeen police stations of the district to the extent of four times. The experiment proved beyond a reasonable doubt that even though same numbers of incidents of crime were committed, prior to the experiment the police resources were spent on suppression of crime figures but now they were being spent on furtherance of the"rule of law" thereby resulting in disposal of a higher number of cases. The number of cases disposed of after registration of all cognizable offences was more than double than what it was prior to the experiment.

Earlier, minor offences were overlooked and offenders were let off without registration of cases against them. This emboldened the offenders to commit more crime and increased the severity of their crime thereby creating more law and order problems in the future. Mr Tripurari states that, "the spectrum of the crime pattern indicates that the proper implementation of law by the police may prove to be more effective and beneficial in the prevention of the offences rather than use or demonstration of force by the police."

Another startling result of the experiment was that though there was not any considerable increase in the instances of false complaints or arrests, the number of people who surrendered before the court of law went up by four times. The number of convictions in a court of law also doubled. The increased number of surrenders and convictions ended up saving valuable resources and time of the police.

The success of the experiment can be attributed to the fact that the experiment instilled professionalism in the police whose primary job is to enforce the"rule of law" as per the procedure established by law.

Sec 154 of CrPC

It has to be noted that Mr. Tripurari was not acting in any extra-judicial manner while conducting the Jalpaiguri Experiment. He was merely implementing Section 154 of the Criminal Procedure Code. Section 154 of the CrPC states, "Every information relating to the commission of a cognizable offence, if given orally to an Officer-in-charge of a Police Station, shall be reduced to writing by him or under his direction, and be read over to the informant; and every such information, whether given in writing or reduced to writing as aforesaid, shall be signed by the person giving it, and the substance thereof shall be entered in a book to be kept by such officer in such form as the State Government may prescribe in this behalf."

According to the National Crimes Record Bureau, India has around 165 cases registered in a year on average per 100,000 persons, as opposed to upwards of 7,500 cases in many developed countries. If these figures are to be believed as a true indication of the prevalence of crime then there is much less crime in India than in Sweden which reports 14,900 offences per 100,000 persons.

The table below gives a very good illustration of crime statistics in some of the countries:

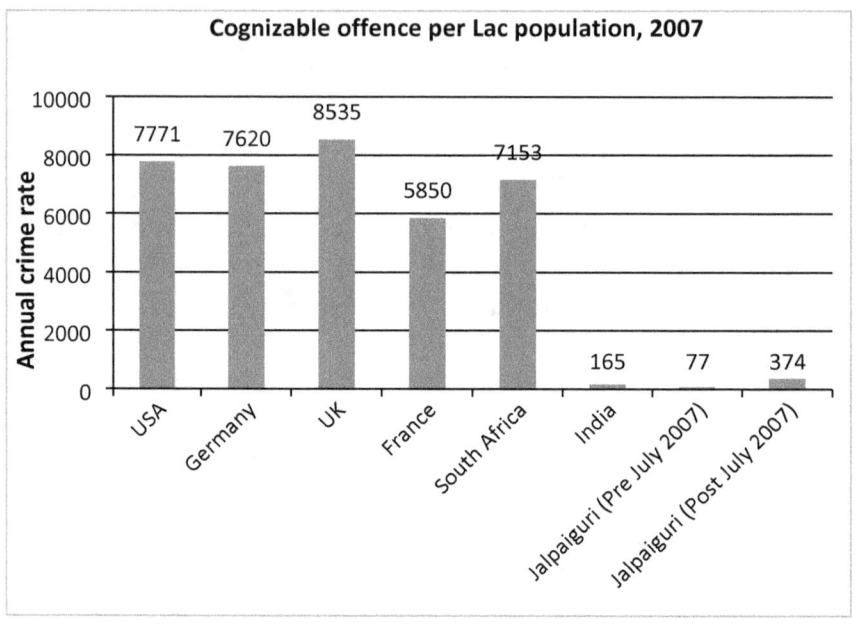

"Police in India frequently fail to register crime complaints, called First Information Reports (FIRs) and to investigate crimes. Police officers told Human Rights Watch that they are often under pressure from political leaders to show a reduction in crime by registering fewer FIRs. Some said that they face suspension or reprimand if they register too many. Police also blame their failure to investigate cases on insufficient personnel and a reluctance to take on new cases that add to an already heavy workload." - Human Rights Watch

Apart from "burking" some of the other malpractices associated with the registration of FIRs, are:

- Non recording of a complaint
- Minimising the gravity of the offence, for example, recording a robbery as a burglary or a burglary as a theft
- Falsely recording, implicating, filing an FIR for extraneous reasons

Taking serious note of "burking" various courts in the country, including the Supreme Court, has said that the police force is mandated to implement the law by following its procedure. The police are not legally competent to change the processes of law, neither are they supposed to stop or alter them.

Factors assisting Burking

Superior officers tend to judge their junior officers on number of cases outstanding. This incentivizes the Station House Officer (SHO) and Duty Officer from not recording or understating the commission of cognizable offences. It may be mentioned here that the number of cases pending for investigations is, most of the time, used as a thumb rule to measure the efficiency and capability of any police officer. Less number of pending cases is correlated as a reflection of good police work whereas their large number is equated as a failure on the part of the police officers. Constant pressure to keep the crime figures makes the police get into the habit of suppression of crime or "burking" in police parlance. The concept of burking can be easily explained as the denial or refusal on part of the police to register the First Information Report (FIR) when an aggrieved party comes to the police station.

A general temptation of attaching undue importance to the number of pending cases sometimes compels the police officers to indulge in all sorts of extra-legal activities so that the number of pending cases could be restricted to a minimum possible level. In this regard, the "golden practice" prevalent is to ensure that the present pending figure remains less than the corresponding figure of the last period. Since the number of pending cases being directly proportional to the number of cases recorded, all available means are adopted to avoid the recording of cases. The local nexus involving police and various other interest and pressure groups plays a major role at this stage. The complainant is sometimes influenced so that the gravity of offences could be minimized, for example, from dacoity to robbery, from robbery to burglary, from burglary to theft. In a nutshell, the process of law is subverted to achieve the target of less number of pendency of cases.

Most of the police officers usually find themselves stifled between the two opposing interests: enforcing the "rule of law" and, at the same time, managing the crime figure at low level. This predicament is one of the main reasons for the suppression and minimization of the crime figure at the Police Stations.

This has helped the offenders or criminals only; alienated the public from the police and given scope to outsiders to interfere. Respect and fear of law has gone away, the Criminal Justice System is being seen as a farce and lawlessness has become the hallmark of our society.

The CrPC makes the SHO the centre of policing in his area. The powers given to the SHO require him to be a highly evolved, fair and ethical individual. This position of great discretion and responsibility at the frontlines of policing can be subjected to abuse with impunity, by officers who have the wrong mindset. Transparency and fairness in the functioning of the Police Stations is at the core of effective policing. Arbitrariness by the police displayed, more often than not, at the time of registration of a cognizable offence, makes it most difficult to put into practice the "rule of law" as enunciated under Section 154 of the CrPC, as a consequence of which the foundation of the Criminal Justice System gets severely damaged. The first and probably the most important stage where this "rule of law" stands negated at the time when the cognizable complaint is not registered at the Police Station.

Although a police person, who is supposed to investigate crime, has to be highly trained in the area of investigation, he or she is woefully undertrained and overworked. This leads to the tendency at the Police Station to refuse FIRs to reduce the work load.

The police have not received incremental resource allocation, technology up-gradation and training that they desperately need to meet contemporary challenges. Crumbling infrastructure also contributes to burking.

Also we must keep in mind that the Indian Penal Code, 1862 and the Criminal Procedure Code, 1898 (though amended in 1973 and thereafter in a piecemeal fashion every couple of years) are essentially the legislation of an oppressive and racist colonial regime interested in shackling the native populace of their fundamental rights and zealously guarding against the slightest challenge to its authority. Burking is essentially a continuation of that mentality and sadly is still prevalent in our policing.

The judicial process in India is seen to involve procedural complexities, high cost and inconvenience of litigation, and delayed delivery of justice. In the absences of any semblance of speedy justice, the natural tendency is to turn away the victims who approach the police for help in recording their complaints.

Effects of Burking

Lack of authentic data on crime: It is shocking to be aware of the fact that we, as a nation, DO NOT possess authentic crime statistics, owing to avoidance of FIR registration or minimization of crime over generations.

In the absence of minor offences being recorded when they are committed, petty criminality is allowed to grow unchecked.

We feel that free access of ordinary citizens to the Criminal Justice System through the route of compulsory recording of FIRs at Police Stations, will firmly establish and uphold the"rule of law" required by a democratic and modern civil society. Particularly the weaker sections have been denied access to justice over generations in an independent India.

Policemen who engage in burking and get into the role of dispensing instant justice without FIR registration and proper investigation, suffer from mental uneasiness and stress, since this modus operandi can cause, and surely does cause, grave injustice as well. The lack of role clarity also confuses the rank and file and distracts them from investigation.

Documentation of the experiment

The "Jalpaiguri Experiment" has been reasonably well documented and provides the empirical basis for the conclusions drawn by this document.

To be able to analyze the importance of the success of the "Jalpaiguri Experiment, one has to take a careful look at the profile of the district. It is one of the oldest and largest of the 18 districts of the state of West Bengal. It borders Nepal, Bhutan, Bangladesh and the districts of Siliguri and Koch Behar on the east and south. The district is demographically largely rural with a few towns. Large parts of it are covered with forests. There are potential law and order problems arising from the activities of Gorkhas (advocating a separate Gorkha state), Kamtapuris (advocating a Greater Koch Behar state encompassing Jalpaiguri and Koch Behar Districts and parts of Assam), Adivasis (who work on the extensive tea estates) and the Maoists. In such difficult circumstances

Mr. Tripurari was able to demonstrate the validity of the Jalpaiguri Experiment by maintaining law and order and also providing social justice to the weaker sections of society by providing free access to the criminal justice system.

Misuse of Sec 41 of CrPC

In no way was the Jalpaiguri Experiment done by misusing the power of arrest that is given to the police under Section 41 of the CrPC.

Section 41 of the CrPC states: "(1) Any police officer may without an order from a Magistrate and without a war rant, arrest any person-

(a)   Who has been concerned in any cognizable offence, or against whom a reasonable complaint has been made, or credible information has been received, or a reasonable suspicion exists, of his having been so concerned; or

(b)   Who has in his possession without lawful excuse, the burden of proving which excuse shall lie on such person, any implement of house-breaking; or

(c)   Who has been proclaimed as an offender either under this Code or by order of the State Government; or

(d)   In whose possession anything is found which may reasonably be suspected to be stolen property and who may reasonably be suspected of having committed an offence with reference to such thing; or

(e)   Who obstructs a police officer while in the execution of his duty, or who has escaped, or attempts to escape, from lawful custody; or

(f)   Who is reasonable suspected of being a deserter from any of the Armed Forces of the Union; or

(g)   Who has been concerned in, or against whom a reasonable complaint has been made, or credible information has been received, or a reasonable suspicion exists, of his having been concerned in, any act committed at any place out of India which, if committed in India, would have been punishable as an offence, and for which lie is, under any law relating to extradition, or otherwise, liable to be apprehended or detained in custody in India; or

(h)   Who, being a released convict, commits a breach of any rule made under subsection (5) of section 365; or

(i) For whose arrest any requisition, whether written or oral, has been received from another police officer, provided that the requisition specifies the person to be arrested and the offence or other cause for which the arrest is to be made and it appears there from that the person might lawfully be arrested without a warrant by the officer who issued the requisition.

Any officer in charge of a police station may, in like manner, arrest or cause to be arrested any, person, belonging to one or more of the categories of person specified in section 109 or section 110."

The recent amendment in Section 41 of the CrPC, has tried to restrict the arbitrary use of power of arrest by the police in connection with offences punishable with imprisonment of seven years or less.

Policing is a law-enforcing process wherein the use of "minimum irreducible force duly sanctioned by law", sometimes, becomes inevitable under some unavoidable circumstances. It may be needless to mention here that force which has got no sanction of law should never be used for policing for quite obvious reasons.

The frequent use of even the "minimum irreducible force" in a day to day policing may not be a desirable thing for a civilized society. The frequency of the 'use and demonstration of force' for policing may be a barometer to measure the presence of"rule of law" in a particular society at any particular time and place. The lesser the frequency, the better it is and the ideal situation may be envisaged as of "policing without using force".

Need for reforms

Modern day India is facing a completely different threat perception today than it was during the times the Police Act and all the subsequent amendments were passed and enforced. If we are to take a careful look, the following categories can be envisaged where some form of police or paramilitary assistance is required:

- Terrorism
- Insurgency
- Basic law and order

Conclusion

With the compulsory registration of cases, there is no discrimination between rich and poor. Besides the above mentioned changes which have been projected through the objective analysis of the relevant crime statistics or its related data, the advantages of the compulsory registration of FIR could be perceived in the day to day policing as well. The interference or influence from the vested interest groups or pressure groups at the time of recording of FIR will be reduced to a nil. The mental trauma of the police officers, due to the suppression or minimization of the offences, will be reduced. The nefarious nexus between police, lawyer, politician and touts, operational at the Police Station level and deciding the fate of almost 80% cognizable offences which used to go unrecorded, will become redundant.

The compulsory registration of FIR implied that there was no need to form a group before visiting a Police Station for lodging a complaint, thus giving less opportunity to the public to assemble against the police and to create law and order problem. There was no need for the police personnel to display bad behaviour against public, as they had been left with no discretion to refuse any complaint. The FIR became the most powerful weapon for the police officers to fight crime and to maintain law and order, unlike earlier, when its higher number quite often used to generate a lot of anxiety and fear among them.

The compulsory registration of FIR started bearing a very good impact over general law and order in the Jalpaiguri district as the fear of law was instilled in the minds of trouble mongers and their leaders. Majority of the trouble mongers were taken care of during their honeymoon phase only. It may be noticed that the criminals also start their learning phase by indulging in minor offences like wrongful restraint, threatening, slapping, molestation etc and slowly they graduate themselves when they begin committing major offences like Murder, Rape, Dacoity, etc. This experiment reiterated the fact that there was no one above the law who could provide shelter to any offender, thus minimizing the chances of becoming self-proclaimed dada or don of the area. This experiment tried to establish the professionalism in the police whose job is to enforce the laws of the land as per the procedure established by laws.

The impact on law and order of the district became positive because of the effective implementation of the law.

It needs to be remembered that a long journey cannot be completed without the accomplishment of the first step taken in the right direction. The Jalpaiguri experiment was an expression of the fact that policing, strictly in accordance with the procedure established by law, would be the most practical and the effective way of establishing the "rule of law".

Note on Methodology

1. Field visit and extensive interviews with stakeholders in Jalpaiguri District

2. Field visit and interviews in some other districts of West Bengal, like Coochbehar, West Midnapore, Howrah, North 24 Parganas, etc.

3. Field visits and interviews in other states of India, like Himachal Pradesh, Punjab, Chandigarh, Delhi, Bihar, etc.

4. Interviews with serving and retired IPS officers, leading NGOs, members of the Press and representatives of Industry

5. Interviews with Parliamentarians and Legislators

6. Visits to Police Station and other field offices to study FIR registration

7. Study of secondary sources including commission reports and articles by experts.

Respondents

Respondents: West Bengal

- Sh Asok Mohan Chakraborty, (Retd.) IAS

- Sh A.B. Vohra, (Retd.) IPS, Former DGP, West Bengal

- Sh Bhupinder Singh, (Retd.) IPS, Former DGP, West Bengal

- Sh Ramakrishnan, (Retd.) IPS

- Sh RJS Nalwa, IPS

- Sh Kundalal Tamba, IPS

- Sh Adhir Sharma, IPS

- Sh Zulfiquar Hasan, IPS

- Sh Thayagaraju, IPS

- Sh Arun Prosad Mukherjee, (Retd.) IPS, Former DGP, West Bengal and former Governor of Meghalaya

- Sh Goutam Mohan Chakraborty, IPS, Commissioner of Police, Kolkata

- Sh Nandkumar Saravade, IPS

- Sh R. Ranjit, IAS

- Sh Tripurari, IPS, DC Central, Kolkata Police

- Smt Vandana Yadav, IAS, DM Jalpaiguri

- Sh Anand Kumar, IPS, SP Jalpaiguri

- Sh Kalyan Bandopadhyay, IPS, SP Cooch Behar

- Sh Debaprasad Ray, MLA

- Sh Manohar Tirkey, MP

- Sh Ajay Kumar Nand, IPS

- Sh Hari Kusumakar, IPS

- Sh Manoj Kumar Verma, IPS

- Sh Dhrubajyoti De, IPS

- Sh Santosh Sarkar, Member, CPI(M) District Committee, Jalpaiguri

- Sh Tapan Bhattacharjee, Secretary, Bar Association, Jalpaiguri

- Sh P.K. Bhattacharjee, Secretary, Indian Tea Association, Dooars Branch

- Sh Anirban Dey, Correspondent, ABP

- Sh Ranvir Kumar, IPS

- Sh Hari Kusumakar, IPS

- Sh Narayan Swarup Nigam, IAS

- Sh B. D. Sarkar, O/C, Malbazar PS

- Sh Mrinmoy Roy, Chairman, IIM Calcutta Alumni Association

- Prof. Asok Banerjee, Indian Institute of Social Welfare and Business Management

- Prof. Sougata Roy, Dean, IIM Calcutta

- Sh Nilotpal Mazumdar, Dean, Satyajit Ray Film and TV Institute

- Sh Soumya Ray, CGM WB Telecom Circle, Bharat Sanchar Nigam Ltd.

- Sh Saumitra Mohan, IAS

- Sh U.R. Bhattacharya, United Bank of India

- Sh Vinod Babbar, United Bank of India

- Sh Tapan Bhattacharjee, Advocate, Jalpaiguri

Respondents: Bihar

- Sh Hari Kishore Singh, Former Minister of State for External Affairs, Govt. of India, and Chairman, Bihar State Planning Board
- Sh D. N. Gautam, (Retd.) IPS, Former DGP, Bihar
- Dr. Arvind Verma, (Retd.) IPS
- Sh D.M. Diwakar, Director, A.N. Sinha Institute of Social Sciences, Patna

Respondents: Orissa

- Sh S.S. Dev Dutta Singh, IPS
- Sh Suman Nandi, IIM Calcutta

Respondents: Tripura

- Sh K. S. Subrahmanian, (Retd.) IPS, Former DGP, Tripura
- Sh P. K. Siddharth, (Retd.) IPS, Former DGP, Tripura
- Sh Suhas Chakma, Director, Asian Centre for Human Rights, Delhi

- Sh Subhra Kanti Gupta, Look East Magazine

Respondents: Uttar Pradesh

- Sh Prakash Singh, (Retd.) IPS, Former DGP, UP and Assam

- Sh Ashish Gupta, IPS

- Sh Amitabh Thakur, IPS

Respondents: AP

- Sh Mahesh Bhagwat, IPS

Respondents: Punjab

- Sh Nilabh Kishore, IPS

- Sh Kunwar Vijay Pratap Singh, IPS

- Sh Roopinder Singh, Assistant Editor, The Tribune, Chandigarh

- Sh Shiv Kumar Verma, IPS

Respondents: Rajasthan

- Sh Bipin Kumar Pandey, IPS

- Sh Pankaj Kumar Singh, IPS

Respondents: Karnataka

- Sh R. Srikumar, IPS

- Sh N. Narasimhan, (Retd.) IPS

Respondents: Delhi

- Sh N K Shinghal, (Retd.) IPS

- Smt Maja Daruwala, Director, Commonwealth Human Rights Initiative

- Smt Nawaz Kotwal, Coordinator - Police Reforms, Commonwealth Human Rights Initiative

- Sh Sushil Raj, Program Officer, The Asia Foundation

- Dr. Ashok Dhamija, (Retd.) IPS

- Sh Kamal Kumar, (Retd.) IPS

- Dr. B.V. Trivedi, Bureau of Police Research and Development

Respondents – Madhya Pradesh

- Raghuveer S. Meena IPS

Respondents: Himachal Pradesh

- Sh B. N. S. Negi, IPS

- Sh Sonal Agnihotri, IPS

- Smt Nandita Gupta, IAS

Respondents: Maharashtra

- Sh Satya Swaroop, New Media

- Sh Devdutt Modak, IIM Ahmedabad

Selected Bibliography

- Article on "Jalpaiguri Experiment" by Sh Tripurari, IPS, published by BPR&D

- "Broken System: Dysfunction, Abuse and Impunity in the Indian Police" by Human Rights Watch Report

- Commonwealth Human Rights Initiative Advocacy Paper on "Police Act, 1861: Why we need to replace it?"

- Police Act, 1861

- The draft Police Bill, West Bengal

- PRB, West Bengal

- PRB, Punjab Haryana and HP

- "Police Executive Relationship in India" by Sh Kamal Kumar (Retd.) IPS

- "FIR Registration" by Dr. Ashok Dhamija (Retd.) IPS

- "Lies, Damned Lies and Statistics" by Sh N. K. Shinghal (Retd.) IPS

- CAG Report on "Police Modernization"

- Commission on Centre State Relations Report: Volume V on "Internal Security, Criminal Justice and Centre-State Cooperation"

- Writ Petition (Civil) No. 310 of 1996 (Decided on 22.09.2006); Prakash Singh and others vs Union of India and others

- Thomas Committee Minutes: "Monitoring Committee: Supreme Court Order (16-05-2008)"

- The Code of Criminal Procedure, 1973

- "Report of the Malimath Committee on Reforms of the Criminal Justice System – some observations" by amnesty international

- Malimath Committee Report: "Committee on Reforms of Criminal Justice System"

- Draft Report on "National Anti-corruption Strategy"

- "The Grammar of Anarchy: Who can say how the people of India and their political parties will behave" by Dr. B.R. Ambedkar.

The Police Station At the Vanguard:

Study for Kolkata Police by Pan-IIM Alumni Association

Project Brief: Pan IIM Alumni Association in Kolkata intends to engage with the Government and the community at large. At the invitation of the Commissioner of Police, the association has interacted with O/Cs and Additional O/Cs of Police Stations and other senior ranks of Kolkata Police.

The Police Station is at the vanguard of policing....observations and recommendations follow...

Report structure:

1. Observations from Workshop on Behavioral Management

2. Observations and Recommendations on Systemic Change at the Police Station

For detailed notes please refer to the Annexures I and II.

Observations from Workshop

(I) Leadership

• Leadership Quality, as it happens in any organization, is not uniformly distributed. Although some of the participants have shown good leadership quality, most of the chosen leaders were not upto the mark

• Concept of Leadership in their minds is traditional. The focus on leadership has shifted from skill orientation to seniority and position.

• Some chosen leaders took a long time in comprehending the issues in some of the exercises. Both because of lack of comprehension and lack of communication ability Briefing given by Leaders to the group was poor

• Individual Initiative is discouraged which stifles the dynamism of an able junior

• Communication Gap exists between IPS and non-IPS officers leading to lack of development of initiative among non-IPS officers

• Deep-seated collective assumption about the nature of hierarchy existing in the police force. A Hierarchical Organization with a rigid structure discourages development of leadership

• There is difficulty in differentiating between Power based on Legitimate, Task-related Authority and use of power unrelated to task and role

(II) Teamwork

• Hierarchical organization with a Command and Obey system is not conducive to development of proper teamwork. In the absence of a designated leader no consensus could be arrived at for taking task-related decisions. Lack of total group involvement was observed during many of the exercises

- Listening and Communicating Ability needs to be developed further in order to improve teamwork

- There seems to be a Communication Gap between PS chiefs and the higher authorities

- Lack of Down to Top Communication also impedes proper teamwork

- Competitive rather than Collaborative Approach was chosen by all the groups despite clear choice given to adopt collaborative approach. Collaboration was easier with colleagues known over a long period of time than with other colleagues

- A clear Lack of Trust between various groups also emerged in some of the exercises

(III) Time and Stress Management

• Delegation of Authority as a concept is not seriously practiced. Lack of collaborative approach with distributive authority lead to process delay and inability to complete the task at hand within a given time limit.

• Overwork and inadequate rest lead to loss of sense of time leading to stress. Because of nature of their work where one working day merges into another the concept of time tracking does not exist leading to poor time management. Inability to grasp complex issues under pressure of time.

• Lack of Trust and Candor as values lead to overloading oneself with work and this also leads to create enormous stress at work.

- Lack of Proper Working Environment and Facilities in professional and personal life lead to stress.

- Absence of Time for Self and Social Life also add to stress.

(IV) Conflict Resolution

- Top to bottom Nature of Organization where a person at the bottom is not assured of being heard lead to enormous internal conflict.

- IPS-non IPS Divide is also a source of conflict at the bottom. Non-IPS officers feel that they are not generally addressed and treated properly.

- Lack of Collaborative Approach led to conflict amongst groups to the detriment of everyone concerned. Groups found it difficult to rise above small interest in order to achieve bigger gain. As a result quite often everyone ended up loser. This was displayed by some groups.

• Lack of Distributive Authority affected resolution of conflict.

• Due to the nature of work pressure, Social Interaction between colleagues of even many years is near zero.

Recommendations on Behavioral Change and Stress Management

Summary Observation: Given the nature of hierarchy and because of their 24X7 nature of job O/Cs and Addnl. O/Cs have lost touch with their internal resources.

Recommendations on systemic changes:

1. Work to be properly organized so that 24X7 nature of the duties of O/Cs and Addnl. O/Cs is removed (reference Bangalore Police)

2.   The Residence of the O/Cs and Addnl. O/Cs should be as close as possible if not attached to PS

3.   Install training department and training centre for Behavioral training with budget and Annual Training Calendar.

4.   Creation of a Yoga Centre and Recreational Facility at every   PS.

Recommendations on Behavioral Change and Stress Management are given in Annexure 2.

Recommendations on Training and Counselling:

1.   To bring change we recommend a package comprising of the following:

A.   Conceptual inputs on Development of Personality and Identity to be followed by Experiential Learning Events.

B. The experiential learning events will be based on work with small groups based on the Tavistock Institute Model and Social Sensing Matrix which has been used in India quite a few times.

C. This will be followed up by a number of Indoor and Outdoor Exercises for focus and experiential learning.

D. Behavioural Inputs to IPS Officers is also to be given to remove communication gap.

2. After taking care of general stress resulting from 24X7 schedule it is possible to organize Counselling Sessions for individuals who nonetheless feel stressed.

Police Station: Observations and Recommendations

Based on feedback from O/Cs; Addnl O/Cs

    I.   Staffing

    II.   Duty Hours of Personnel

III.   Infrastructure

IV.   Recruitment, Promotion and Posting

V.   Work Culture

VI.   Training

VII.   Operations

VIII.   Role of Media

IX.   Public Interface

(I) Staffing

Observation

•   Constables/ ASIs unfit for promotion are posted in PS which is the face of the force. Thus PS does not have good investigators

•   Inadequate force at PS. Police/ public ratio is adverse

Recommendation

- Direct Sub Inspectors (not Promotee) should be posted in PS in reasonable number

- Increase in number of force with proper training

- Radio Flying Squads to be brought under direct control of PS for better monitoring

- Sense of responsibility to be improved in lower levels

- Involvement of all ranks in work in PS

- Easier access to experts in investigation of cases where specific expertise is required

(II) Duty Hours of Personnel

Observation

- Erratic duty hours, sometime 16-18 hours a day

- No weekly day off

- After night duty, same routine the next day. Deployment of force after performing night duty is inhuman

- Family members are denied of support even in emergencies

- Poor physical fitness and health condition

- Poor response to public owing to overwork/ fatigue and disturbed personal life

Recommendation

- Compulsory weekly time-offs

- Rest may be given to force after night duty

- Police should enjoy Puja duty-off by rotation

- Identify and stick to core functions

- Health check-up for force on

(III) Infrastructure

Observation

- Poor accommodation for constables – WWII barracks

- Poor quality of food at barracks

- Ill-equipped personnel - no shoes for rainy season

- Working condition is not favorable - no place for officers to sit/ rest

- Transportation/ vehicle shortfall remain an acute problem

- No provision for maintenance of vehicles

- Posting far away from place of residence

Recommendation

- Lodging at Barracks and PS to be improved

- Good canteen facilities to be provided

- Adequate vehicles in good condition are required

- Provision to be made for maintenance of vehicles

- Housing to be provided at PS of posting

(IV) Recruitment, Promotion & Posting Observation

- Recruitment is faulty

- Posting and promotion policy is not transparent but erratic

- Eligible candidates are getting one/ two promotions in lifetime

Recommendation

- Recruitment should be based on:

1. moral values and right attitude

2. physical condition,

3. intelligence,

4. educational qualifications and

5. family values

- Posting and promotion should be on merit-cum-seniority, with more emphasis on merit. This will remove frustration and apathy and will improve morale and efficiency

- Promotion can be based on qualifying through courses or exams

- Pay to be uniform for performing the same job Police Station

(V) Work Culture

Observation

• Lack of respect and trust between superiors and subordinates

• Unnecessary interference for normal day-to-day work and over supervision lowers scope for decision-making on the ground

• Supervisors ask for implementation of impossible orders. Often superior officers do not have field experience or are not in touch with ground reality

• Bogus complainant having no evidence are seriously entertained

• There is the widespread practice of passing the buck to junior officers when something goes wrong

• Subordinates flout orders of superiors

Recommendation

- Respect , trust and camaraderie to be developed across all ranks

- Autonomous functioning to be allowed at different levels with checks and balances

- Proper incentive/ recognition for individual/ group achievements

- Superiors to listen to grievances of staff

(VI) Training

Observation

- No facility for Training for all ranks in the force

Recommendation

- Regular training for all levels

- Basic and Refresher courses

- Attitude and behavior of trainers need to be correct

- Training of O/Cs and Addnl. O/Cs in management

- Pre-promotional training for SIs

- Sufficient exposure to entire spectrum of policing duties before promotions

- Mandatory computer skills training for all staff

- Focus of training methods and contents

- Periodical re-training is required:

- Explosives

- Scientific aids to investigation

- Evidence Act

- People management

- Handling stress

(VII) Operations

Observation

- Collection of intelligence is poor

- Poor record keeping

- No de-briefing system

- Lengthy documentation for FIR

- No contingency fund to meet day-to-day expenditure

Recommendation

- Recommendations of BPR&D to be implemented

- Modernization of communication system

- Computerization to remove scriptory work

- Increasing awareness of Criminal Justice System

- Imprest account to be provided to every PS

(VIII) Role of Media

Observation

- Egocentric rather than work centric desire to have super cop image

- Role of media in creating image larger than life

Recommendation

- Credit to deserving staff in Newspaper/ Media.

- Staff not to be abused in front of public

- Credit to be given to the teams and not the individuals

- Press briefings to be done by the designated spokesperson

(IX) Public Interface

Observation

- Non-registration of Complaints owing to:

1. Increase in scriptory work

2. Fear of increase in numbers

3. Political interference

4. Corruption

Recommendation

- Compliance with the rule of compulsory registration of FIR to be strictly enforced

- Assessment of competence purely on statistics of crime should go

- Reiterating through directions from the top that there is no choice in matters of receipt and registration of complaints.

- Encouraging public to register cases freely

People-friendly Police Station

1. Police Station should look and feel welcoming to visitors.

2. Police Station should have adequate facilities for seating and sanitation.

3. Helpdesk for women and children.

4. Comfortable area in the Police Station where women and children can make their complaint without fear and in confidentiality.

5. Display posters on the rights of women, children and other members of the public.

Expected Attitude of Police Station staff

1. Should enjoy working in Police Station

2. Should make Police Station more friendly for visitors and police personnel

3.   All personnel in Police Station to treat visitors and complainants with sensitivity and courtesy

4.   Enquiries - whether written or verbal, including telephone calls – to get replied to promptly.

Annexure I: Preliminary Report after interviews of OCs and Addl. OCs of Kolkata Police and Field Visits

Introduction: IIM Alumni conducted a survey on Stress & Behavioral Management of Officers-in Charge and Additional Officers-in-Charge of Police Stations in the city of Kolkata by speaking to a cross-section of present and past officers of the force. Based on the survey, appropriate training is being designed for O/Cs and Additional O/Cs.

Diagnostic Methodology:

- Meeting with Mr. S. Ramakrishnan (Retd.) IPS, Secretary General – Bengal Chamber of Commerce and Industry

- Meeting with Mr. Tripurari, DC - ESD

- Meeting with Mr. Asit Kumar Chakraborty, ACP – South Division

- Meeting with Officers-in-Charge:

- o Mr. Santi Prasad Roy, O/C, Burtolla P.S.

- o Mr. Joyanta Das, O/C, Ekbalpur P.S.

- o Mr. Manoj Kumar Das, O/C, Charumarket P.S.

- o Mr. Tapan Saha, O/C, Beliaghata P.S.

- Meeting with Additional Officers-in-Charge:

  - o Mr. Subhas Ch. Sarkar, Addl. O/C, Hare Street P.S.

  - o Mr. Tapan Kr. Paramanick, Addl. O/C, Narkeldanga P.S.

Field Visit to:

- Burrabazar Police Station

- Hare Street Police Station.

After discussion with Mr. S. Ramakrishnan, we have identified the following training needs:

- Leadership

- Teamwork

- Conflict Resolution

- Time Management

Learnings from discussion with Mr. Tripurari IPS, former SP – Jalpaiguri, and initiator of the Jalpaiguri Experiment:

- Lack of Role Clarity: The role of a Police Officer is to enforce the Law. Today, the reality is that a Police Officer is expected to do much more than the mandated responsibility of "enforcing the Law".

- Lack of Motivation: The average Police Officer is de-motivated from doing his job which can be stated as: "Policing is the process whereby a Police Officer collects evidence regarding commission of offence and submits before judiciary". The de-motivation is owing to the perception that the "rule of Law", and thus the policeman's sincere efforts, would be thwarted by motivated entities.

- The O/C has inadequate resources to discharge the job of: "Enforcing the Law by following the procedures established by the Law using the means available".

Learnings from discussions with O/Cs and Additional O/Cs on 08.06.2009: The points for discussion were as follows:

- Major hindrances in the Policeman's daily chores.

- Idea of one's role.

- Causes for de-motivation, if any.

- How can the situation be improved?

- Do we agree that recording all FIRs is to be done?

- Manage time better.

- Avoid/ manage conflicts.

- Available manpower in the Police Station to be more optimally utilized.

- How can the training course help?

- Any other suggestions.

- Quality of Promotee Officers: Quality of promotee officers (promoted from ranks of Constable, etc.) is poor.

O/Cs are not able to delegate to these officers since they do not deliver the expected output. This contributes to stress on the job.

Suggested Action: Training for promotee officers.

- Stressful Work Schedule: O/Cs have a 24X7 hours job with hardly any holiday.

  Suggested Action: Training in Stress Management, Yoga and Personal Health.

- Reluctance to delegate: O/Cs are reluctant to delegate since they do wish to dilute/ share their powers.

  Suggested Action: Training in Team Work

- Interference in Police Stations: There is a high degree of environmental interference. With the climate of change in the political atmosphere of the state, this interference has started increasing.

  Suggested Action: Officers must have strict loyalty only to enforcing the Law and avoid approaches from vested interests with tact and inner confidence.

- Recognitions: Methodology for nomination to recognitions like award of "Police Medal" is seen as arbitrary.

  Suggested Action: The system of nomination be made transparent.

- Performance of tasks outside the ambit of Constitution-mandated job role: O/Cs often required to perform many tasks which are outside the ambit of their responsibility and for which they have no training or resources. Eg: Restoring of power connections in the aftermath of Cyclone Aila.

- Salary, Amenities and Social Infrastructure: Salary and amenities of the O/Cs need to be improved. Even quantum of petrol sanctioned for the O/C's use is not sufficient for daily use. Living facilities at their quarters and the physical condition of the Police Station leaves much to be desired. Recreation facilities are not available. All these factors contribute to increasing stress.

Suggested Action: There is an urgent need to provide combined office-cum- living quarters for all O/Cs as also proper social amenities for dependents.

- Inadequate Manpower: O/Cs feel manpower is inadequate and over-burdened owing to unrealistic duty hours.

  Suggested Action: One suggestion is to create the post of Senior O/C with several O/Cs under him. Also creation of more Police Stations would ease the burden.

- Relationship between O/C and Addnl O/C: This relationship is often far from cordial and discord between the two leads to lower efficiency of the Police Station. O/Cs are sometimes reluctant to develop their subordinates.

  Suggested Action: Training in Team Work and Mentoring.

- Seniority rather than Merit and Professionalism in promotion: The system emphasizes on seniority rather than merit and professionalism in promotions.

  Suggested Action: If emphasis can be shifted to merit and performance, the force will be a more professional entity.

- Wastage of time in judicial process

Conclusions:

- Training course focusing on Leadership, Teamwork, Time Management and Conflict Resolution

- Monitoring and feedback system to check and proliferate the learnings from above course.

- Provide training on Yoga, Stress Management and Basic Health as a second step.

- Creation of a Training department for taking care of training needs of the force.

Structure of proposed Course:

- Introduction

- Rapport-building:

- Contract between faculty and participants

- Building of confidence and psychological safety

- Discussion of methodology

- Leadership

- Case Study/ Exercise: Management Game

- Conflict Management:

- Case Study/ Exercise: Management Game

- Team Building

- Case Study/ Exercise: Management Game

- Time Management:

- Case Study/ Exercise: Management Game

- De-briefing

- Write down Learnings

- Record the Learnings.

Annexure II: Report on 4 one-day diagnostic workshops for the OCs andAddl. OCs of Kolkata Police - By Prof. Gouranga Chattopadhyay

Genesis of the Workshops: The PAN IIM Alumni Association had invited the Commissioner of Police (CP) for an interactive session, at the end of which the latter requested the Association to undertake a diagnostic study of the OCs and Addl. OCs of Kolkata Police Stations to locate behavioural problems related to leadership, time management, stress management, etc. This study was to be done in order to suggest fresh inputs in police training.

Three members of the Association, Messer Mrinmoy Roy (MR), Jhelum Chowdhury (JC) and Sanjay Tantiya (ST) initially interviewed several OCS and submitted an interim report to the CP. During this period Dr. Kakoli Saha of ISABS was also associated in some way with the project. Thereafter the CP requested MR and JC to design a one-day workshop to make an in-depth study and submit a report. He further suggested to rope in Emeritus Professor Gouranga Chattopadhyay (GC) in this project since he had extensive experience in working on the behavioural problems of Kolkata Police from traffic sergeant level (project sponsored by Concern for Kolkata with assistance from a private company) in 1995 to OCs and Addl OCs in 2000 (sponsored by Bengal Chamber of Commerce). This project was also supposed to cover Officers in the level of DCs to the Jt. Commissioners. But the DCs did not like the idea of working on 4 continuous weekends soon after heavy duty for other work. So the then CP, Mr. Bajpai cancelled further work. However, a report was drawn up and submitted, on the basis of which some changes were introduced in the force.

After a couple of meetings between GC, MR, JC and ST (with KS attending the first meeting) it was decided that GC would design a suitable workshop and four such workshops would be held. Each workshop will have 24 participating OCs and Addl. OCs.

GC would direct the first two workshops only as he had other commitments later on in the month of July 2009. MR and JC would handle the last two workshops.

The following behavioural processes were observed during the workshop:

Communication gap of serious nature exists between the police station chiefs and the higher authority manned by IPS officers. The nature of this gap reflected some kind of cavalier attitude on the part of the IPS officers expressed towards their non-IPS cadre. While the workshop consultants had given a note on the nature of the workshops along with a whole-day schedule and had requested the authorities to circulate it among the prospective participants, the majority of them had no idea of why they were asked to report at hall dedicated to the women family members of police officers on a particular day at 9 AM and for how long. They arrived in drib and drabs and the workshop on all the 4 days could be started at least half an hour late. Further, roughly 20% of the prospective participants (about 4 to 5 out of expected 24) never turned up. Some of them stated that they expected to go back to "duty" (obviously they did not consider attending a workshop as part of their duty) in about an hour's time. However, fortunately they accepted the word of the consultant and fully participated up to 5.30 PM, as noted in the schedule. On being pressed about this lack of communication, they stated that there was nothing uncommon about it, since the IPS officers considered themselves as a cut above the others and this was also reflected in the way they were generally addressed and treated. Further this was also reflected in the pay scales when non-IPS officers rose to levels, which were by and large meant for IPS officers only. The non-IPS officers of the same rank, doing similar work were paid less.

Since to them the most important tasks center around the work of their respective police station jurisdictions, and they did not get the schedule and GC's write up, most of them had had taken their own time to report at the workshop venue, which, as mentioned earlier, resulted in staring late every day.

Each day the work began with personal introductions. The model was set by the consultants who freely gave information about their work life, their family life etc. Then the participants were asked to spend ten minutes in pairs of their own choice. Each person in the pair would have to question the partners about themselves and take notes. At the end of 10 minutes, each person will introduce his partner to the others. This exercise revealed the fact that due to the nature of their work pressure, as also (as perceived by the consultants) being treated by their super ordinate role holders not as individual human beings but as a porridge mass of subordinate role holders, social interaction colleagues of even many years were near zero. It was for the first time that they exchanged information about each other as human beings with existence beyond the role of an inspector of police. The consultants felt that this behaviour could be changed in order to get rid of certain destructive consequences (mentioned later) through intensive Team- building exercises that would incorporate sessions also for greater understanding of the assumptions police officers make about themselves almost unconsciously. The teams for these workshops should be made up of both IPS and non-IPS officers and last for at least 4 days, since the idea of quick and instant learning is a fantasy devoid of real life experience!

The first exercise, designed to bring out issues of trust and collaboration, showed one of the negative impacts alluded to before. While they could collaborate with colleagues known over a long period in work life, they had difficulty in collaborating with other colleagues. This showed that long association and past successful collaborative experience and helpful behaviour demonstrated again and again by one of the colleagues led to building of trust that the structure of the force did not encourage. Team building workshops mentioned in point 3 above could also change this behaviour.

The second important thing that came out of this first exercise of the day was a deep-seated collective assumption about the nature of hierarchy existing in the police force. This assumption was about absolute rigid nature of the structure in which individual commitment to task and the capacity to take initiative and leadership beyond hierarchic situation of ordering subordinate role holders had little meaning, since ambitious juniors were seldom even listened to with any respect. In other words, individual brilliance in terms of skill in quick decision-making, risk taking and leadership were ignored.

The next important finding was that they had little notion of delegation of authority. This was perhaps largely because trust and candour as values were missing. This would also, obviously, impact on the officers by creating enormous stress in work. Each person would almost automatically overload oneself with work as well as harbour feelings of probable attack from others.

The above factors led to the feeling of frozen hierarchy in which each officer felt self-important. As a result they find it difficult to listen to colleagues (and may be subordinate role holders as well) when cooperation and pulling in resources of others as thinking individuals. They got angry at each other with noise level increasing, making difficult for a person to giving sound advice when it was important to keenly listen to colleagues in order to succeed in joint performance of the task in the second exercise. This exercise had built-in issues of clear communication in absence of seeing the others who also engaged in the same task and that of trust combined with collaboration in the absence initial absence of data. It further underscored their difficulty in trusting inputs by colleagues whom they could not see. Mutual trust and openness were casualties.

In both the time-bound exercises they failed to manage time through either not appointing a colleague as time keeper in the first exercise or by for getting that the consultants would tell them about the passage of time if they asked for it during the second exercise. We would like to make an assumption about this failure to manage time on the basis of other data that emerged from both what they had mentioned in the interviews earlier and some of the statement that they made during the current series of diagnostic workshops. Unlike in any other organisation dealing with tasks in the social milieu of the Indian society, in the Kolkata Police Force the OCs and Addl. OCs, who hold quite seriously responsible position that require quick

difficulty in differentiating between power based on legitimate, task related authority and the use of naked power unrelated to task and role.

The third and the last exercise of the day was on surfacing the problems related to managing conflict resolution. In the situation created by design all the participants found it difficult to distribute authority for task methodically collaborate managing conflict to complete the task on time. Actually this was one exercise that the completed successfully on time, But this happened because certain individuals took leadership and others sort of apathetically sat around and talked in sub-groups. It seemed to reflect a continuous situation of anxiety in the participants' lives that they sought to handle by training themselves (obviously unconsciously) to withdraw from situations that they cold convince themselves as of minor importance since others were there to take care of the problem.

It is possible for the consultants, led by GC, to organise workshops to surface, reflect upon and work through various kinds of behavioural problems lodged in the structure of the force, as experienced by the OCs and Addl. OCs in these one-day workshops, excepting for the issue of time management. That initially and primarily require the police force to work out how all officers can avail of at least one day of complete holiday each week.

The workshops referred to in point 12 above have been successfully tried out in many commercial organisations and NGOs by GC. Time required for each workshop is clear four and half days of residential work. The location, in order for those to be meaningful, has to be outside Kolkata in places like, for e.g. Gorumara, where facilities exist for such programmes.

Overall it appears that given the nature of hierarchy and because of their 24X7 nature of job they have lost touch with their internal resources. In order to change this trend our

~

recommendation is conceptual inputs on development of personality and identity to be followed by experiential learning events.

The experiential learning events will be based on work with small groups based on the Tavistock Institute model and Social Sensing Matrix which has been used in India quite a few times. This will be followed up by a number of indoor and outdoor exercises for focus and experiential learning.

Until training is also given to IPS Officers, communication gap is bound to happen.

After taking care of their general stress resulting from 24X7 schedule it is possible to organize counselling for individuals who nonetheless feel stressed.

A special note: In the early 1990s GC had held workshops for the IPS at the Hyderabad Campus. There he found that the trainees worked for 12 hours or more each day, seven days a week, alternating outdoor work and indoor concept sessions. The outdoor work made such merciless demand on the physical and mental capacities of individuals that many of them slept through the first 2 or 3 days of concept sessions. This was also clearly known to the teaching staff, yet it continued. One wonders to what extent the experience of "merciless" training schedule of the IPS officers is projected on their immediate subordinates, who are mostly OCs and Addl. OCs of Police Stations. As it happened, during one such work related visit, GC came across a Detective Chief Inspector of Scotland Yard in the Hyderabad Campus. He was doing research on the state of police training in various former British colonies. He said that he was appalled because in the present day police training in UK, they worked from 9 to 5 with 5-day week! So one wonders to what extent the travails of Indian Police (and also of Indian bureaucracy) emanates from an unexamined hangover of the colonial era. In a recent article I have dealt with this

phenomenon at length. It is entitled "Colonialism-in-the-Mind".

Annexure III: A suggested checklist for People friendly Police Stations

Structures

- Does your police station (PS) look and feel welcoming to visitors? Do you have adequate facilities for seating and sanitation?

- Does it have a helpdesk for women and children? If not, is there any comfortable area in the PS where women and children can make their complaint without fear and in confidentiality?

- Does your PS display posters on the rights of women, children and other members of the public, as well as the Mission Statement of Kolkata Police?

Procedures

- Does the Crime Board in your PS include a separate list of crimes against women and children?

- Do you maintain the statistics of crimes against women and children in a separate register? Do such cases get reviewed periodically? What is the follow up action taken?

- In cases of serious physical injury to a woman or a child (a Cognisable Offence), is a case registered immediately?

- Do you give an acknowledgement of every petition? If a case is filed, do you always give a copy of the FIR to a complainant?

- Has there been any case of abuse of power by a police personnel, especially related to women and children, in your PS? If so, what was the action taken?

Attitudes

- Do you enjoy working in your PS? How can you make it more friendly for visitors and police personnel?

- Do all personnel in your PS treat visitors and complainants with sensitivity and courtesy?

- Do enquiries – whether written or verbal, including telephone calls – get replied to promptly?

- Do all police personnel in your PS believe that violence against women and children is unacceptable? Do they understand that in most cases of violence, a complainant comes to the police station as a last resort?

Resources

- How many police personnel (men and women) in your PS have participated in workshops and refresher courses on sensitising police towards violence against women and children? Do these police personnel share their experiences with the rest of the police station?

- Is there any reference material available within the police station on violence against women and children?

Community Connections

- Is your PS involved in people-friendly/community activities? Do you organise or conduct community meetings with the local neighbourhood watch? How often do these meetings take place? How many people attend?

- Do you know/visit the NGOs that work in your area, especially with women and children? Do you display a list of local NGOs/clinics/hospitals/prominent citizens who offer shelter, medical aid, counselling services and/or legal advice? Do you refer complainants to them if required?

- Are there any community outreach programmes on women and children in which your PS, the community groups and the NGOs work together (e.g. meetings in schools, colleges, slums etc)? What is their impact?

- Do you ask for a social worker or local NGO person to be with a child, in cases of children in conflict with the law?

- Has there been any report in the media of your police station and its work? Was this a positive or a negative report?

Centralizing the Investigation function

An intriguing resource allocation problem which Police Reforms grapples with is the separation of the Investigative and the "Law and Order" responsibilities at the Police Station.

Investigation of crimes and maintenance of law and order are two separate functions requiring skill sets and resources which are quite different. An investigator of crimes has to sift through evidence, speak with witnesses, prepare a charge-sheet and then participate in court proceedings. Maintaining law and order, more often involves standing guard at innocuous places and filing suo moto FIRs if the circumstances so warrant. Police Reforms Commissions have therefore very correctly recommended that the two functions be separated at the Police Station level.

However, in achieving this separation at undermanned and under-resourced Police Stations across the country, the problem arises on the manner in which manpower and resources be optimally split up between the two functions. Suppose there are three inspectors and eight sub-inspectors in a rural Police Station with jurisdiction over about one hundred square kms. Two inspectors and five sub-inspectors, let's say, are allocated to solving crimes. That leaves one inspector and three sub-inspectors to maintain law and order among two hundred thousand people inhabiting thirty villages. What if now criminal activity declines but the area faces a land agitation? The investigators will be under-utilized while those responsible for law and order will find themselves over-stretched.

One way out of the situation is to centralize the investigating function and move it out of the Police Station altogether. In each Police District, the investigative department can be based at the SP's office. In the cities, the investigator may be based at the DC's office or at the head quarters of the Commisionerates.

"Investigating" SHOs can conduct the investigation of crimes, backed by a specialized team of sleuths and supported by a greater concentration of tools for investigation. There can be more effective liaison with the Forensic departments and probably also with the Public Prosecutors in the courts. There is also scope for more meaningful exchange of intelligence and learning within a more compact team.

In the Police Stations, the SHO can focus only on maintaining law and order. He also needs to ensure that all FIRs are faithfully recorded and transmitted to the investigating team for further action. All ranks below the SHO at the Police Station will be focussed on only maintaining law and order. Also they can engage more on intelligence gathering in the locality as well, now that they are freed from undertaking investigation.

This can have the effect of significantly reducing the shortage of infrastructure and resources at the Police Stations. There would not be further need of maintaining records of cases and evidence at the Police Station.

On the other hand the healthy effects of centralization of a specialist role will show in greater effectiveness in solving crimes.

The investigating teams can be developed as centres of excellence, with adequate training inputs and cutting-edge technology.

Scarce trained investigative resource will be deployed optimally where crime has occurred. A common knowledge pool of case histories will further improve effectiveness.

Possibly it's time to do this.

Opportunity for Bihar

Shri Nitish Kumar deserves our *pranam* and heartiest congratulations on his return as Chief Minister with the overwhelming mandate of the electorate.

The first task of governance is to ensure the rule of law. In his first innings at the helm of the state, he restored the "rule of law" in Bihar. After suffering from lawlessness and anarchy over generations, the common man could again walk safely on the streets. The mafia dons were put behind bars and their power crushed. Junior officers and engineers in the state government were empowered to make governance more efficient and check corruption at higher places. The process can be continued to make Bihar the role model for policing in the country.

It needs to be ensured that the police stations compulsorily record all offences reported to them. This will make the criminal justice system accessible to one and all, irrespective of socio-economic, gender and caste disparities. This effort would make the state par excellence in protecting the life, liberty and honour of its citizens.

Once Bihar is universally accepted as a safe place to live in, the economic resurgence of the state can be focussed on. A start has been made earlier by facilitating the creation of infrastructure like highways. Some industrialists have also been invited to start new projects primarily in the areas of food processing and renewable energy, although that has mostly remained at the level of projects sanctioned. However initiatives are now required which would touch the rank and file and create strong internally sustained growth.

Universities like Nalanda and Vikramshila in Bihar were the IITs and IIMs of ancient India. Although these universities have long ceased to function, education has continued to remain uppermost in the priorities of the people of Bihar.

Parents overlook their privations to ensure education for their children. Unfortunately, owing to the uncertain environment in the state and the dismal situation of local educational institutions, they have to perforce send their children to study outside the state. Generations of Biharis have been studying, working, spending and investing outside their home state. As a ballpark, one-fifth of the one hundred million population of the state comprise the youth. A significant part of Bihar's youngest and brightest are studying and living outside the state. Those who cannot afford higher education outside the state, drop out of school after class ten, the standard until which they are assured of a midday meal in school, and join the migrant labour force. Assuming that ten per cent of Bihar's twenty million youth, that is two million students, are able to continue their higher education outside the state, at an average expenditure of Rupees Two Lacs, this translates into an annual outflow of Rupees Forty thousand Crores. It is time now to reverse this flood by making quality higher education available within the state.

A beginning was made in primary education by equipping the girl student with the basic and convenient mode of transport, namely the bicycle. While continuing the initiative in primary education, the time has now come to bring about a renaissance in higher education. The improved law and order situation offers a convivial environment for that today.

New centres of educational excellence would require limited land and capital expenditure compared to heavy industry. There is also abundant supply of teachers available to teach at such new institutions. It is estimated that the capital city of Patna can support at least five institutes of higher education, whether in engineering or medicine or computer applications. Other satellite towns can support two such institutions each. Twenty thousand students in each university, with an annual expenditure of Rupees Two Lacs per annum per

~

student translate into a turnover of Rupees Four hundred Crores per university. Support services to the teachers and students would lead to the growth of ancillary services around each such educational centre of excellence. Such growth of the service industry around educational institutions would start attracting the migrant Bihari labourer back to the state.

Responding to the larger volume of demand for goods and services, industry will on their own accord start installing new production capacity. This will lead to a demand led industrial resurgence.

The renaissance in higher education in Bihar will lay the foundation for the state's future economic prosperity and would stand the country in good stead in the years to come. It is our earnest hope that Bihar can thus emerge as the engine for growth in the country.

A Kemalist vision for Pakistan

Aiming towards achieving and maintaining complete separation of Church and State, aka post WWI Turkey, the following are proposed:

Nationalism to be dissociated from any kind of religious identity or affiliation

Change the name "Pakistan" to "Freeland", Indusland", etc. which has no religious, sectarian or ideological connotation

Federal Capital:

Change the name "Islamabad" to "Indus City" or suchlike

Else shift administrative functions to an urban area unencumbered by historical baggage and reflecting inclusiveness and plurality in its name. This is analogous to the shifting of the erstwhile Ottoman capital from Constantinople/ Istanbul to nondescript Ankarra

More radically, do away with a physical capital, let the government of this entity become a portal: www.indusland.in

Strict disouragement of public exhibition of one's religious beliefs:

Enforce western dress and clean-shaven well-groomed appearance in all public places; mandatory for all employees and affiliates of the government

Any symbols of religious adherence to be strongly discouraged in public

The laique state not to recognize any religion

The state not to fund any activity remotely religious in nature. On the contrary the state to actively promote:

- Compulsory liberal education in English

- Patronage of art and architecture

- Encourage the scientific temper in all discourse

Modern Criminal and Civil Justice sytems to be put in place. All legislation to follow in letter and spirit the Universal Declaration of Human Rights and other enlightened international covenants

Introduce Swiss-style referendum on issues of national debate, without compromising on the core principles

Minimise governmental involement with the economy and allow entrepreneurship to flourish.

The above wishlist may sound preposterous at this moment, and I may have intentionally digressed from the topic of proposing specific policies which the GOI can adopt to engage with the current entity. But drawing a broad vision at some stage might put the picture in perspective.

I also console myself by imagining that Mr. Iqbal's dreamy ideology of the 1930s may have had a similar halo of poetic fancy in its time. Unfortunately his dream had prevailed over the principles his contemporary Ataturk had used to overcome a failed Caliphate. This, as a historical aberration, somehow needs to be undone.

Demolishing the idea of "Pakistan" should be the sole and inexorable agenda of India, vis a vis the western neighbour.

One milestone was reached in 1971 with the creation of Bangladesh on linguistic lines, though the initial advantage in that new state may have been utilized sub-optimally.

The practical steps I propose are:

Unrelenting military containment

Taking the "nukes" out. Active international canvassing to denuclearize and disarm Pakistan

Entente with Central Asian Republics, USA, Russia and China (?)

Supporting legitimate struggles for self-determination in Pakistan

Propaganda campaign demonstrating the preponderence of the concept of "India"

International canvassing to reduce/ cut off western aid, claiming accurately that it feeds the NGOs and does not percolate downwards

Internally reform politically and economically so that India can legitimately showcase its commitment to individual freedom, democracy and the free-market to the western world

Allow educated and skilled Pakistani professionals to work in India on special visas, so that the elite there becomes economically dependent on INR inflows and aspires to living and working in India. Intensely monitor and impose restrictions on Pakistanis living in India to prevent any of them from engaging in subversion. Provide politial asylum to professionals trying to flee Pakistan

Allow entry of bright Pakistani students in Indian universities, so that the Pakistani youth aspire to getting educated and live the "good life" in India. Introduce GRE/ GMAT style entrance exams for them

Allow Pakistani capital to be invested in India, or facilitate such investments to be routed through India

Become the "financial center" of south Asia, attracting not only skilled Pakistanis, but also increasing number of western expatriates, thus also controlling the cashflows in and out of Pakistan.

US downgrade – opportunity INR?

"The old order changeth, yielding place to new, And God fulfils himself in many ways, Lest one good custom should corrupt the world..." – Idylls of the King

The facts of the situation are as below.

The world economic order as evolved after the 1944 Bretton Woods agreement is coming undone at the seams. The hegemony of the US, whether through domestic profligacy, weak politics or international adventure, is slowly but surely unravelling.

The S&P downgrade of the US sovereign rating, on the back of months of uncertainty over repayment crisis, leaves Canada as the sole AAA+ sovereign entity in the Americas. With the faltering of the New World, the Old World also has its share of chills and shivers, with at least two of the PIGS (Portugal, Italy, Greece and Spain) facing real prospect of default.

The declining fortunes of the US economy, makes it critical for its largest creditors to provide it succour. It also begs the question: can alternates be developed to the US Dollar as a store for value and as currency of international trade and investment?

There has been an increasing flurry of activity among market-watchers in the BRICS (Brazil, Russia, India, China and South Africa) to put forward the case of their respective currencies as an alternate to the US Dollar. Among these, the claim and efforts of China seems to be the most credible. Indeed, "Dimsum Bonds" have started catching the imagination of treasury heads.

However, the current market for other sovereign bonds is so much more limited than that of US Treasury Bills. Hence it will take time for the "Dimsums" to offer the level of credibility, functionality and scale that US T-bills have provided since over more than sixty years.

The possible decline of the US Dollar will probably see the eclipse of London as the largest financial centre of the world. London had achieved this position on the back of the Eurodollars flooding into European reconstruction after World War II. It remains to be seen who proactively captures the Remnimbi transaction flows in the years to come. Possibly it will be Hong Kong SAR, Shanghai or Singapore, in the Chinese hinterland, but it is too early to read the signs.

Where does this leave the INR?

Not very well placed, it seems.

India is a struggling developing economy, with poor political leadership, poor energy resources and an S&P rating of BBB-. Since the early nineties, it has become increasingly susceptible to global hot money flows and very much tied to the fluctuating fortunes of mainly western export markets. In a sense it is otherwise like the closed states of Myanmar and North Korea with the additional distractions of balloting every five years, some exports and a weakly efficient capital market.

India's overpopulated urban conglomerations, Mumbai or Kolkata, are for reasons unknown, but possibly owing to myopic planning, not yet ready to emerge as global financial centres.

How does the US downgrade affect India?

Firstly the "feel good" factor based on external stimulus would go. No more the export growth riding on US domestic demand, the boom in the capital markets based on capital inflows from the west, the H1B facilitated diaspora of the wannabe middle-class to hipper climes. The Indian economy will have to innovate harder to identify and develop viable domestic markets and seek newer export niches in the highly competitive and non-English speaking oriental markets of Greater China, as also those of emergent Africa and Latin America.

Secondly, India will have to move painfully away from its engagement with the US-led world to a more Sino-centric one. That might mean not only holding Remnimbi denominated foreign exchange reserves as opposed to US Dollar assets, but building meaningful bridges of friendship and collaboration with an erstwhile competitor in the interests of greater commerce and world peace in an increasingly China-centric state of affairs.

Thirdly, India might like to take advantage of the opportunities in the world of finance. That means not only developing its own global financial hubs but also appreciating and possibly taking advantage of the changes in money management brought about by stricter US legislation. The Dodd Frank Act of 2010, introduced in response to the financial crisis of 2008, has effectively forced a veteran trader like George Soros into retirement. Broadly it has become difficult, if nigh impossible, for Hedge funds to operate in the US, in the manner that they did earlier. Since global funds still require management, and possibly they are looking at a more comfortable base, is there an opportunity that India might like to look at? A set of convivial regulations, which keeps control, but does not smother enterprise, could just push the business of managing global funds into India.

India needs to continue to have a long hard look at all that is not quite right: dependence on fossil fuel, the fiscal deficit from uncontrolled spending on doles, supply-side causes for inflation and endemic poor governance and red tape. These issues have been around for a long time now, and as yet there are no solutions in the horizon. Indeed there is an increasing realization by the people that they may need to reform the structure of their polity. This is probably a job that needs to be done in a hurry, since the new order of things will not provide much breathing space to laggards.

The new world throws up opportunities for the brave and challenges for the unprepared.

The probability is low that INR would emerge as a global reserve currency or India as a destination for global capital in light of the steady decline of the former hegemon. Nonetheless, these are worthwhile objectives towards which India at least can strive towards. The road is uphill at the present, as the world swings from the western hemisphere to the far-east. In the interest of self-preservation in the midst of these strong external forces, India needs to reform and rediscover its own identity, and do that fast.

www.ingramcontent.com/pod-product-compliance
Lightning Source LLC
Chambersburg PA
CBHW062004280526
45787CB00005B/1988

* 9 7 8 1 5 1 8 7 4 8 7 9 0 *